MW01179099

Mindfulness for Children

Teach Mindfulness to Kids and Teens

By

Louise Waghorn

An Introduction to Mindfulness

Mindfulness is one of the most powerful tools you can give anyone, let alone the children in your life. It provides a sense of well-being, reduces instances of stress, anxiety, and depression, improves focus and productivity, improves self-esteem, relationships and boosts creativity. As a teacher for over eleven years and now a devoted Aunt, I immediately saw the need to bring the benefits I was experiencing myself through my own mindful practice to the lives of kids and teens.

In this book, aimed at parents, teachers and anyone who works with children, I provide a brief overview of mindfulness, before looking at why mindfulness is so beneficial for kids and teens in today's world. I outline the benefits of mindfulness, before sharing practical ways to teach mindfulness to children of all ages. In the Mindfulness Meditation section, various examples of meditation exercises are explored, with detailed directions to provide a guideline for developing a mindful practice that fits the needs of your children. In the remaining section, I look at ways to incorporate mindfulness into life at school, home and by making mindfulness part of your daily routine.

In many ways, this book is the tip of a much bigger iceberg, but I hope that it will empower you to make mindfulness part of you and your children's lives and empower you to explore the potential of mindfulness. Throughout this book, I provide references to resources that I've found useful, and I encourage you to think of this book only as the first step of your mindful journey.

What is Mindfulness?

Mindfulness is being present in the moment. Whatever you're doing—walking, brushing your teeth, breathing—you are one hundred percent focused on it. Have you ever been playing sports, reading a book, or hanging out with friends, and completely lost track of time because you were so caught up in what you were doing? If your answer is yes, you've experienced mindfulness.

Focus is key no matter what you're doing—studying, training or interacting with family and friends. You already turn off your cell phone when you've got a big project to work on. What if you could do the same with those annoying, distracting thoughts that fill your mind when you try to concentrate? What if you could silence those nagging doubts, negative self-talks, and comparisons that always leave you depressed? You can—with mindfulness. It doesn't take much imagination to see how mindfulness can enrich your life—and your children or your students' lives.

Practicing mindfulness on a regular basis has been proven to improve the mind's capacity for concentration. You'll be more focused on whatever you're doing. You'll also be more appreciative and thankful for the good things in your life. You'll be more in tune with your emotions. And by introducing your child, teen or students to mindfulness, you'll be helping them unlock all their potential.

Mindfulness originated in Buddhist tradition but has been adapted by psychologists to meet the demands of modern life. Since the 1970s, following the studies led by Jon Kabat-Zin, clinical psychology and psychiatry have used mindfulness to reduce stress and anxiety, help treat depression and improve health and wellbeing. Practicing mindfulness on a regular basis has been proven to improve breathing, lower blood pressure, and reduce anxiety. It also helps users to recognize their emotions and take control of them.

Despite mindfulness's Buddhist origins, you don't need to be spiritual to enjoy the benefits of being more aware, better in tune with your emotions, and more relaxed. All you need to practice mindfulness is as open mind and as little as ten minutes a day. Fortunately, children with their sense of wonder and freedom from preconceptions about the world, are already mindful (and teenagers are already adept at questioning your judgment...). All you have to do to foster an enriched sense of well-being is to help them tap into abilities they already possess. In fact, as you explore mindfulness together, you may find that it is the children in your life who teach you.

Practicing Mindfulness

Mindfulness can be practiced in a number of ways. The most common of these is through meditation. This reflects the origins of mindfulness in Buddhist practice. Sitting meditation is the most common, but you might find writing or walking meditation works better for you or your child. When starting meditation it is helpful to focus on an object— your breath, your body, or an object in front of you— for example. Over time, you can expand your awareness to your body, your surroundings, and your thoughts. You'll notice improved concentration, a greater sense of well-being and improved self-awareness. Other ways to practice mindfulness include simply by setting aside some time every day to invest an everyday routine or moment with awareness, writing or drawing, or applying yourself fully to conversations with friends and family.

Unlike most after-school activities, mindfulness requires no uniform, special equipment, or pressure. If your child can't fit a mindfulness activity into every day, try every second day. Mindfulness can be practiced anywhere, anytime. You can use it at home with your child or teen, encourage them to use it at school or on the sport's field, or in your classroom at school. It can become part of your daily before school routine or the last thing you do before you switch out the light at night. Use it before a big test, an important game, try-outs or the first day at a new school. It can last from one minute to as long as you want.

Mindfulness can also improve relationships. By taking the time to listen to a close friend or family member with undivided attention, you're not only practicing mindfulness but you're strengthening relationships, too. This may be the hardest to teach a self-conscious teen, but by focusing on the moment, not what they think their peers might say or think, they'll learn the importance of listening. And by receiving your full attention, they'll feel valued and more confident.

Mindfulness is most effective practiced on a daily basis. The more often you use mindfulness techniques, the more effective it is. Just like any skill, you get better from regular practice. Each time you meditate, the neural pathways in your mind are rewritten. This allows you to achieve a focused state more easily, and experience deeper levels of relaxation. Regularly checking in with your thoughts and emotions keeps your self-aware and able to deal with life's unexpected surprises. Make mindfulness part of you and your child's daily life, and you'll give them a tool that will carry them through the challenges of school, college and beyond.

Why Mindfulness is So Important to Kids and Teens

The Challenges Facing Young People Today

Today's young people face a myriad of challenges in life, at home, at school, and within their social circles. Technology is a persistent intrusion into daily life. Bullying at school and the problems of peer pressure remain a serious problem, as do the pressures created by school exams, sporting competitions, and the media. No wonder more and more young children are being found to suffer from anxiety and other stress-related problems.

In this environment, mindfulness is even more important. It can counteract the distracting effect of social media, provide students with the confidence and strength to make healthy choices in life, and the freedom of mind to succeed at their academic and sporting goals. For them to succeed, they need positive—and mindful—role models. As parents and teachers, you play a critical part in your children's development.

Technology

Today's generation of young people has never known life pre-internet. From Day One, they've been surrounded by TV, video games, and social media. Many live life through the screen of a smartphone. We don't know yet what effect this dramatic shift in the level of technology in our lives will have on our children. What we do know is a child's environment has a dramatic impact on their attention span.

Just like muscles must be exercised through constant use, the attention span must be used in order to be developed. Different activities work the attention span in different ways. Reading requires children to focus on one book for sustained amounts of time. Watching TV, on the other hand, offers the brain a quick succession of visual stimuli. The brain is less engaged, requiring TV shows to up the ante. The internet is even more of an attention grab, with bite-sized pockets of information or entertainment competing for viewer's attention. Although beneficial in many ways, the effect of a steady diet of TV and internet leads to increasingly fragmented attention spans at the age when the brain is doing most development. This directly impacts a child's learning ability.

Bullying and Peer Pressure

Despite concentrated efforts to stamp it out, bullying remains a constant problem facing students in schools across the world. Despite the best efforts of teachers and parents, most children will experience some form of bullying during their school career. Bullying is insidious in whatever form it takes, and leaves the victim isolated, stressed and struggling with feelings of low self-esteem and anxiety, and in extreme cases, leads to depression, self-harm, and suicide.

Increased peer-pressure is another impact technology has on children and teens. Social media is now ever-present. Though Instagram, Snapchat, Messenger and Facebook, teens are constantly connected to a wide circle of peers. This means that it is easier than ever to bully someone anonymously. It is difficult to hold internet trolls accountable for their actions, and their victims feel utterly powerless and unable to escape them, no matter where they go.

Our children also face increased danger from online predators, the accessibility of porn, and the popularization of the dangerous use of drugs and sex in popular media. If children and teens are to survive these threats, they need self-confidence, awareness of their own value and the ability to manage their emotions to avoid manipulation.

Internal Pressure

For teens and young adults, internal pressure to succeed can create an additional source of stress. While internal motivation is key and we should encourage our children and students to set goals for themselves, we must be careful not to imply any judgment. When pre-exam nerves result in stomach cramps, or a child feels that they've disappointed their parent or teacher by not being smarter/a better baseball player/prettier, these internal pressures have created an external problem.

The problem is especially difficult for girls. Due to the presentation of unrealistically thin models as 'normal' and the constant photoshopping practiced by the beauty industry, we have a very warped idea of what constitutes 'normal' for women. In fact, a survey conducted by Macquarie University revealed that we no longer recognize what a healthy weight for women is. Instead, the participants of the survey thought 'underweight' was 'thin' and 'thin' was healthy. Faced by constant propagation of unrealistic images of beauty by TV shows, commercials, and even their peers, girls put immense pressure on themselves to achieve the unachievable. They may become ashamed of their bodies, and unwilling to discuss their fears and anxieties.

Gay, Lesbian, Queer, Trans, Asexual and other non-gender-binary youths face a complex set of challenges, too. These groups are more prone to bullying, and that problem is compounded by the fear of being rejected by their families as so many youths tragically are. A mindfulness practice can't eliminate bullying, but it can help a child to develop the peace of mind, resilience, and clarity to resist and achieve their full potential.

Children's Brain Development

Every day there's a new and contradictory piece of advice on how to raise your kids, or how to reach out to a struggling student. If the constant barrage of expert advice wasn't overwhelming enough, neuroscience is showing conclusively the effect that good parenting—or the lack thereof—has directly on a child's brain development. The early years are particularly important as this is when the child develops his or her stress response system. An overactive stress response system can lead to many problems in later life, including depression, anxiety, illness, inability to form emotional connections, lethargy, and phobias and obsession.

Many of us have an overly romanticized view of our own childhood—or an overly critical one. This makes it hard to clearly evaluate our children's needs. We may dismiss children's emotional distress with statements like 'I always wore hand-me-downs, and I turned out fine.' What we need to remember is that often children don't have the vocabulary to express their very real fear and distress. If they don't have an outlet, they may respond by withdrawing emotionally, internalizing their negative emotion or suppressing it. According to Margot Sunderland, 'about 2 in every 100 children in the US are taking antidepressants, and the World Health Organization reports that depression in adults will soon reach epidemic proportions.' We may be entirely unaware of the difficulties our child is facing until their fear manifests itself in inexplicable stomach pains, or we witness their first anxiety attack. Fortunately, mindfulness gives children tools with which to process their emotions and deal with stress.

Teenagers' brain development

In addition to growth spurts, the appearance of hair in odd places, mood swings and dawning sexual awareness, teenager's brains enter a new period of development. During these years, the prefrontal cortex enlarges, a process that continues into the mid-twenties. The prefrontal cortex is the part of the brain that deals with logical decision making. It governs things like making plans, multi-tasking, prioritizing, organizing thoughts, evaluating the consequences of an action and controlling impulses.

The teenage years are also the period where much of a person's identity is formed and consolidated. As part of discovering who they are, a teenager makes choices that may alarm a parent. Relax! Experimenting with new ideas and taking risks are all part of the teenage experience. Encouraging a mindful habit in your teen can help them navigate this potential minefield without going to extremes. By questioning in a thoughtful way the assumptions they have about the world, teens are less likely to push back reactively against restrictions. And while you may not be able to avoid every poor fashion choice or error in judgment, a self-aware teen is more likely to learn from the experience, less likely to brand him or herself 'a failure.' As teens prepare for the future, facing uncertainty about everything from career choices, to university, to embarking upon romantic relationships, mindfulness is invaluable in meeting the fears and challenges of life head-on.

The Benefits of Teaching Mindfulness to Kids and Teens

Benefits of Mindfulness

Many of us struggle with stress ourselves, and the difficulty of helping our children or students with their own stresses can feel like another impossible burden. It doesn't have to be like this. In fact, by reading this book, you're already taking a positive step to reducing the amount of stress in your life and your child's.

Mindfulness is already having a positive impact on the lives of children. Dr. Addie Wotton, CEO of Smiling Mind, a non-profit that leads the way in using mindfulness in schools to pre-empt later problems of mental health, led an investigation into the effects of mindfulness in children's daily school routines. The students reported improved sleep and fewer cases of bullying and classroom disruptions. Students described as 'more at-risk of emotional difficulties' found they experienced 'improvements in emotional wellbeing, reduced psychological distress, enhanced positive wellbeing, enhanced ability to manage emotions and improvement in concentration.'

The benefits don't stop here. The academic performance of the 1853 students involved in the study improved, with the 104 participating teachers reporting improved engagement with lessons and emotional wellbeing. Outside of academic settings, the Mindfulness-Based Stress Reduction (MBSR) programs pioneered by Jon Kabat-Zim, has been used to combat a wide variety of stress based disorders, from chronic illness to PTSD since 1979, all with positive results. Mindfulness isn't merely the trend of the moment. It is a practice born in centuries of tradition, grounded in neuroscience. While we are still learning all the ways mindfulness can impact our lives, this is certain: you have nothing to lose by trying it, and everything to gain.

The good news.

Young children are already mindful, and they take to mindfulness with an ease that us older types envy! With fewer preconceptions about the world, they'll struggle less with questioning previously held beliefs and look curiously at the world and themselves. By now the benefits of mindfulness should be obvious, but you might still hesitate. What are you worried about?

It is not too late to introduce your child to mindfulness. In her book, The Science of Parenting, Margot Sunderland makes the following claim: 'parents can dramatically influence systems in their child's brain that are key to the potential for a deeply fulfilling life.' Sunderland is talking about the effect of daily interactions of parents and children and their effect on the child's brain development, but she might as well be talking about mindfulness. Frequent meditation actively rewrites the links in our brain. It weakens the pathways between the medial prefrontal cortex and the insula and amygdala, the sensation and emotion centers of the brain—responsible for the 'fight or flight' response. Meditation also strengthens the link between the lateral prefrontal cortex and the medial prefrontal cortex, meaning that we are more likely to respond to a situation with thought rather than reflex. Mindfulness practices have been as effective in improving the lives of senior citizens as they have been for younger adults—and many studies have proven the benefits of mindfulness to students at schools with a daily meditation practice. One million school children across Australia have embraced mindfulness and are enjoying decreased stress, and increased productivity and confidence.

Importance of Role-Models

In all our concerns about the reckless behavior of celebrities, the glorification of sex, violence and substance abuse in movies, games, music, and other media, it is easy to forget that the role-models with the biggest influence on our children are their parents and teachers. The single most effective way to encourage mindfulness in your child or students is to welcome mindfulness into your life.

I strongly recommend spending a month implementing the mindful techniques introduced into this book before teaching them to your child. You'll be familiar with meditation practices, and aware of what works and doesn't work for you—so you'll be better equipped to give your child guidance as they work out what works best for them. You'll be calmer and more accepting of other perspectives so that you'll be better prepared to meet resistance gracefully. With any luck, the benefits of your mindful practice will already have been noted by your family, who will be curious and eager to join you.

Also, consider that the first step in taking care of your child is taking care of you. A frazzled, stressed parent is more likely to snap than offer support and understanding. By keeping you present in your interactions with your child, mindfulness not only allows you to gain clarity and perspective, but it allows you to enjoy your children. Amongst the pressures of balancing work, relationships, and parenting, it is easy to forget how precious each interaction with our children is. Try mindful parenting, and you may be surprised at the difference it makes to your health and happiness.

With these points in mind, the advice that follows is given with the assumption that you will be joining your child or children on their mindfulness journey, not simply giving instructions. 'Do as I say, not as I do' has never been an effective form of instruction—I think we can all agree on that! And with so many benefits that can only really be understood through experience, there is really no better way to teach mindfulness than to experience it yourself.

What do you need?

All you need to teach mindfulness is yourself, your child, and a few moments in which to breathe.

That's it.

Of course, a quiet room free of distractions and ten to fifteen minutes to meditate is great—when possible. As your knowledge of mindfulness grows, you may wish to experiment by signing up for a meditation course, investing in a yoga mat, or keeping a mindful journal. All of these are options, not necessities. Mindfulness is about what happens within your mind. The most precious investment in mindfulness you can make is not costly equipment or a dedicated meditation room, but your time.

Mindfulness Meditation

Why meditate?

Meditation and mindfulness are often assumed to be the same thing. In actual fact, meditation is just one of many ways to practice mindfulness. As Ellen J. Langer states in her book Mindfulness: 'Meditation is a tool to achieve post-meditative mindfulness.' By stilling the mind, concentrating awareness on the natural rhythms of the body, sounds in the surrounding area, or your own breathing, meditation encourages you to experience the ordinary in a new or deeper way. Once your meditation is finished, you bring that heightened awareness, sense of calm, and renewed focus to whatever activity you engage with next.

Another way to look at meditation is as mindfulness training. Mindfulness means being fully present in the moment and giving your full attention to what is happening. Easier said than done. No matter what you or your child may intend, your minds wander. How many times have you walked into a room, only to realize that your thoughts have strayed so far, you no longer remember why you entered the room? How often has your child drifted into a daydream as they sit at their desk, contemplating their homework? Meditation is basically practicing bringing wandering thoughts back to the task at hand. This will help your children develop the skills they need to focus in the classroom, during the big game, or when facing that driving test.

The best way to teach meditation to young children is by sitting down with them and doing it together. Chose an age appropriate guided meditation, or read one of the scripts in the sitting meditation out loud. Older children and teens may feel self-conscious and prefer to practice alone in their room. Work out what works best for your family. Even when you're not practicing meditation together, I believe that it is a good idea for the parent or teacher to meditate too. Not only are you an important role-model for your children and students, but you'll enjoy all the benefits of mindfulness, yourself.

What is the best way to use meditation?

Many mindfulness advocates recommend starting your day with a five to ten-minute meditation. Just like eating a solid breakfast sets you up for a full day of work or play, making mindfulness part of your morning routine ensures that you are more focused throughout the day. Invite your family to consider what time you will designate as meditation time, and talk about why it is important. Be flexible and willing to compromise if necessary. Showing your children that their opinions matter and that they have some control over how they practice mindfulness, will make mindfulness seem more relevant to them.

As you gain mastery of meditation, gradually increase the time you spend on it. The optimum amount of time spent meditating seems to be 25 minutes—but if you can't find this time in your daily life, don't sweat it. Even as little as a minute a day will have an effect.

Another way to get your family on board with mindfulness is by getting them to compare how they feel before and after a meditation session. Get small children to draw a face indicating how they feel before the meditation. For older children ask them to rate their happiness, alertness, and calm on a scale of ten. After you've completed the meditation, ask them to do show how they feel now, and compare that to before they did the meditation. This shows your children how mindfulness can benefit them. Not only will this encourage them to continue with mindful practices, but it sets them up for a good day at school or home. The simple act checking in with your emotions, state of mind and self-means you are more likely to nip a 'terrible, horrible, no good, very bad day' in the bud, or, at the very least minimize the consequences.

Meditation at School

Starting the school day with a short class meditation has been proven to dramatically improve student's retention of the day's classes, participation in the class and engagement with the teaching material. A regular mindful exercise has even more far-reaching results, extending to improved physical health, lower stress levels and decreased depression amongst students. Primary and secondary schools in Australia committed to exploring the potential of mindfulness took this a step further. Teachers led their homeroom class is a five-ten minute meditation at the start and end of the school day. In addition, every class started with a fifteen second to one minute long meditation. The benefits were immediate and measurable, with fewer instances of bullying, and more engagement in classes.

When teaching meditation to kids and teens, the keyword is to remain flexible. Sometimes, it is just not going to be possible to fit it into your schedule. When that happens, don't beat yourself up, or blame others. Take a deep breath and let it go, committing to trying again another day. Likewise, if your child finds it difficult to sit without moving, don't insist on them staying absolutely still. If Lila can't sit without jiggling her leg, accept that as part of Lila's practice. If you can't concentrate with Lila jiggling, use the sound as the basis for your own meditation, or try again on your own once the kids have gone to school. Sitting meditation will not work for everyone. Experiment with walking or writing meditation until you find something that works for you.

A Final Note on Meditation

Don't expect too much at the start. Just like any other skill, meditation is improved by practicing. Just as you will find your thoughts intrude into your meditation at first, your children will find it difficult to concentrate. For younger children, staying quiet might be the hardest part! Keep in mind that there is no failure in mindfulness. When your mind wanders, acknowledge that thoughts are what your mind is best at. Acknowledge the thought, and return your mind to your meditation. Encourage your children to forgive themselves when they get off-track and reapply themselves. This simple message of persistence without judgment is just as useful to your child or student's self-esteem and attitude to new things as the meditation practice itself.

Sitting Meditation

An Introduction to Sitting Meditation

Sitting meditation is the most common meditation. Chances are you are already picturing a bald-headed monk in an orange robe, sitting cross-legged on the bare floor of some distant monastery. Actually, sitting meditation can be practiced while sitting in a chair with your feet on the ground, sitting on a cushion on the floor with your feet out in front of you, or even lying on your back. The important thing is only that you're comfortable and that you can breathe easily.

A quiet place is good, but if you have a busy house or classroom, just make it as free from possible disruptions as you can. Turn off TVs and cell phones, put a 'do not disturb' sign on the door, and make sure everyone has got that drink or used the bathroom beforehand.

All of the meditation advice that follows are examples meant to be adapted to fit your family or classroom's needs and your particular style. Just as mindfulness opens our eyes to the many possibilities around us, use these as your starting point to practice meditation with your kids and teens. At the end of this book, I will share resources I have found useful, that you can explore to learn more about meditation for kids and teens.

Simple Sitting Meditation

(suggested time: one to two minutes for young children, three minutes for ten-year-olds upwards and five minutes for teens and adults).

Sit in a chair with your back straight and your feet on the ground, or sit on a cushion on the floor with your feet out in front of you. Take a moment to get comfortable. If you want, feel free to lie down.

When you are ready to begin, shut your eyes (if you are worried about falling asleep, keep your eyes half-open). Take three deep breaths, bigger than you would normally take. On the third breath, let it out very slowly. Now, make your breathing normal again. Notice how it feels to breathe. Concentrate on feeling your breath in the rise and fall of your stomach, or as it comes in and out of your nose or mouth. Choose one place and concentrate on it. Focus on the sensation of breathing. Is every breath the same as the last? Do you notice any differences?

Your mind will wander away from your breathing. Each time it does, recognize that your mind is trained to think. Gently bring your attention back to your breathing. To help you focus, you might like to count one when you breathe in, two when you breathe out.

When the time goes, before you open your eyes, take a minute to notice how you feel. Do you feel sleepy, like you've woken up from a nap? Maybe you feel rested and ready for action. You will most likely feel calm. Thank you body for the gift of breathing and open your eyes, ready to go on your way.

Simple Body Awareness Meditation

(suggested time: two to three minutes for young children, four to five minutes for ten-year-olds upwards and five to ten minutes for teens and adults)

Lie on the floor with your arms spread out either side of you. Take a moment to get comfortable. If you need extra support, feel free to get a pillow. If you are worried about falling asleep, keep your eyes open and focused on the ceiling as you do this exercise.

When you're ready to begin, shut your eyes and take three deep breaths. Breathe out slowly, feeling the air leave your body. Let your breathing return to normal. Concentrate on where you can feel the breath coming in and out of your body.

Starting at your toes, let your mind explore all the sensations of your body. Notice where it touches the ground. Can you feel your socks against your toes? If you're barefoot, how does the air feel on your feet? Concentrate on your feet. Are there any unexpected sensations? Be curious.

Slowly shift your attention from your feet to your ankles, up your calves, to your knees and your legs. Notice how it feels where your body meets the floor. Does the carpet tickle? Do you feel sore anywhere?

Your mind may drift. That's okay. It's what the mind does. Just let the thought go, and bring your attention back to your body.

Continue to move your attention up your back, through your tummy, your chest, and your hands. Explore your fingers, your wrists, your arms and your shoulders. Do you feel stiff? Does anything you notice surprise you?

Now it's time for your neck, your mouth, your nose, eyes, ears, and head. As you notice each of these, in turn, pay attention to the sensations you feel. Don't look for certain feelings. Instead, draw your attention to each part of your body and let yourself discover them. If it helps, pretend that you're noticing your body for the first time.

Now, let your attention spread over your entire body. What sensations are loudest? What is your body trying to tell you? Take a moment to be grateful for the hard work your body does for you every day. When you are ready, open your eyes. Go on your way feeling relaxed with increased awareness of your physical state.

Guided Meditation.

A guided meditation is when you follow the instructions given by a meditation leader who is present, or by listening to a recording. There are some excellent guided meditations available for smartphones— see the final section of this chapter. Guided meditations are a great introduction to meditation for you and your child to do together. They are ideal for the classroom, for camps, for sport's teams—the list goes on. You can find guided meditations online or in bookstores, or you can read one of the following scripts out loud to your children.

Many of these scripts contain repetition. It's good to have some consistency between scripts so that the children learn to recognize what is coming next. However, novelty is an essential part of mindfulness. Don't be afraid to go off script occasionally!

Ages 7-12

The following scripts are intended for children between the ages of seven and twelve. They can be adapted for younger or older audiences.

Breathing/Body Awareness

This exercise encourages children to learn to recognize the cues their body is giving them. It uses breathing as the focus of the meditation practice, before moving awareness to the body.

It's time for our special mindful time. Can you lie on your back on the floor? That's right. Put your hands on your tummy and close your eyes. Feel your hands go up and down. What is making your hands go up and down? That's right. Every time you breathe in, your tummy goes up. When you breathe out, your tummy goes down.

Let's take a really big breath. In ... and out. Let's take two more big breaths. In ... and out. In ...and out. Now, let's breathe normally. Feel your hands go up and down. Let's count ten breaths. One... two... three... four... five ... six ...seven... eight...nine ... ten.

Now, imagine you are breathing in a warm, glowing cloud. It settles in your tummy. With each breath, it grows bigger and bigger. Feel it warming your tummy. With your next breath, push it down to your feet. Feel the warm cloud tickling your toes and your feet.

Slowly move the cloud up your leg. Notice how the cloud makes your legs feel warm. With every breath, move the cloud a little higher. Over your tummy. Up your back. Over your chest.

Now feel the cloud move to your hands and fingers. Bring the cloud up your arms. Feel how it warms your shoulders.

It's time to move your cloud to your neck. Feel it warming your chin, your mouth, your nose, your eyes, your ears and your head. Let the cloud sit on the top of your head a moment.

Now, imagine the cloud growing big enough to cover your entire body. Take a moment to notice your whole body, from your toes to the tips of your ears. Let the cloud warm you all over. It's time to say goodbye to the cloud. With your next breath, let the cloud go.

As you breathe out, take a moment to say thank you to the cloud for its warmth, and thank you to your body. Thank you to your legs for walking, thank you to your hands and arms for picking things up. Thank you for your mind for thinking and your body for working.

It's time to finish. When you're ready, open your eyes.

Emotion

This exercise encourages students to realize that emotions come and go. It helps younger children realize they can control what they feel, and learn that emotions arise from a combination of factors.

It's time for our special mindful time. Today, we're going to sit in our chairs. Let's take a moment to get comfortable. Wriggle in your seat.

Are you sitting comfortably? Good. Put your hands on your tummy and close your eyes. Feel your hands go up and down. Every time you breathe in, your tummy goes up. When you breathe out, your tummy goes down.

Can you focus on breathing? Notice how each breath feels. In ... out. If your mind tries to think about something else, tell it 'we're breathing now' and focus on your breathing. You might have to do this a lot. Every time you notice your mind is thinking about something different, focus on your breathing.

Let's take a really big breath. In ... and out. Let's take two more big breaths. In ... and out. In ...and out. Now, let's breathe normally. Feel your hands go up and down. Let's count ten breaths. One... two... three... four... five ... six ...seven... eight...nine ... ten.

Think of something that made you happy. Maybe it was your birthday. Maybe you saw a friend for the first time in a long time. Think about your happy moment.

Now, notice how your body feels. What is different?

This time, let's think of something that made you sad. Picture the moment in your mind.

Now, how does your body feel?

Now, bring your mind back to your breathing. In ... out. In ... out. In ... out.

Feelings, like happiness and sadness, come and go. Sometimes, when we're sad, it is hard to remember being happy. When our feelings get too loud, we can make them quiet by listening to our breathing.

It's time to finish. When you are ready, open your eyes.

Sounds

Just like the breathing meditation, this exercise uses sounds as a focus for mindfulness practice.

It's time for our special mindful time. You can sit or lie down on the floor. Are you comfortable? Good. Put your hands on your tummy and close your eyes. Feel your hands go up and down. Every time you breathe in, your tummy goes up. When you breathe out, your tummy goes down.

Can you focus on breathing? Notice how each breath feels. In ... out. If your mind tries to think about something else, tell it 'we're breathing now' and focus on your breathing. You might have to do this a lot. Every time you notice your mind is thinking about something different, focus on your breathing.

Let's take a really big breath. In ... and out. Let's take two more big breaths. In ... and out. In ...and out. Now, let's breathe normally. Feel your hands go up and down. Let's count ten breaths. One... two... three... four... five ... six ...seven... eight...nine ... ten.

Let's notice the sounds around us. Listen carefully. What sounds can you hear?

Each time you find a new sound, spend a moment listening to it. Try and notice as many sounds as you can.

Listen to the sounds that are a long way away. Slowly, bring your attention to the sounds that are nearest to you. Maybe you can hear a sound that you couldn't hear before.

Bring your mind back to your breathing. In and out. In and out.

It's time to finish. When you are ready, open your eyes.

Ages 13-17

Teenagers have a lot on their minds. They are starting new schools, and facing new pressures. As school work and responsibilities increase, so do the choices they have to make. Not only are hormones playing havoc with their bodies, but their brains have entered a new period of development. The meditation scripts below are designed to help teenagers get some much-needed clarity.

Breathing

A simple meditation exercise using breath as the focal point.

Today, we're going to use breathing to help us focus our minds. First, let's get settled. You can sit in a chair or on the floor. Keep your back straight. Take some time to make sure that you're sitting comfortably. Place your hands on your knees or on your tummy. When you're ready, close your eyes.

Take a deep breath, deeper than you usually take. Let it out slowly. Let's take two more deep breaths.

Now, let's settle into our normal breathing. In ... out. In... out. Place your hands on your tummy. Feel how they rise and fall with every breath you take. Focus on how you can feel your breathing with your hands.

If your mind tries to think about something else, gently bring your focus back to your breathing. You may have to do this more than once. That's okay. Thinking is the what the mind does.

Let's count ten breaths, starting with our next breath. One... two... three... four... five ... six ...seven... eight...nine ... ten.

Now, let's put our hands beside us. Breathe in and out. Notice where you can feel the air come in and out of your body. Chose one place and focus on that.

No matter how many times your mind wanders, keep bringing it back to focus on your breathing. Notice the quality of your breath. Does it feel the same? What differences can you feel?

Let's count ten breaths, starting with our next breath. One... two... three... four... five ... six ...seven... eight...nine ... ten.

We've reached the end of this exercise. When you are ready, open your eyes.

Thoughts

The teenage years are when teenagers start to question their identity. It can be hard for them to view things objectively, and to distance themselves from worries about their peers and the pressures they experience. This exercise helps teens examine their thoughts in a critical way.

Today, we're going to use breathing to help us explore our thoughts. First, let's get settled. You can sit in a chair or on the floor. Keep your back straight. Take some time to make sure that you're sitting comfortably. Place your hands on your knees or on your tummy. When you're ready, close your eyes.

Take a deep breath, deeper than you usually take. Let it out slowly. Let's take two more deep breaths.

Now, let's settle into our normal breathing. In ... out. In... out. Place your hands on your tummy. Feel how they rise and fall with every breath you take. Focus on how you can feel your breathing with your hands.

As you focus on breathing, your mind will wander. That's okay. Today, when you notice that your mind has wandered, step back and examine the thought. Ask yourself: why am I thinking this? Pretend that you are a stranger looking inside your mind for the first time, or a visitor from a foreign culture. Explore the emotional and physical responses to your thought. Now—let it go. Bring your mind back to your breathing.

You can use this technique when you have trouble focusing on your meditation practice, or at any time during the day. Sometimes we react without wondering about why. Opening your eyes to your mind will help you control your thoughts rather than letting them control you.

We've reached the end of this exercise. When you are ready, open your eyes.

Short Meditations

Real life doesn't always allow us five to ten minutes of quiet meditation time. In those situations, the best advice is simply to breathe. You and your child can use these short meditations anywhere. Sitting in the car, on the way to a new school. Waiting to give a speech at the front of the class. Sit down with your child and brainstorm situations that make them feel nervous or tense. Then practice these short exercises for mindfulness on the go.

Take Three.

Three deep breaths that is. If you've been meditating regularly, then your body already associates three deep breaths with a mindful experience. Even when you and your child don't have time for a formal meditation, simply focusing on your breath as you breathe in and out, gives your mind a time-out from internal pressures. You'll be surprised at what a big difference three big breaths can make.

S.T.O.P

STOP is a mindfulness practice that has been around for decades but is still as effective as it was when Dr. Elisha Goldstein, author of The Now Effect, first introduced it. To paraphrase Dr. Goldstein, S.T.O.P encourages you to:

Stop what you are doing.

Take three deep breaths, focusing on your breathing.

Observe your actions, reactions, and emotions. Instead of judging yourself 'I lost my temper! I'm a bad person,' study your reactions: 'My shoulders are tense. I'm breathing rapidly. My thoughts are muddled.'

Proceed mindfully, bringing awareness to your actions.

As you can see, S.T.O.P is useful whenever you discover yourself caught up in a heated moment!

You might feel ashamed by your reactions, especially if you lost your temper with your child. Instead, consider this. If you weren't actively practicing mindfulness, you might not have stopped to consider your actions at all. You did—and you took steps to calm yourself and bring your awareness back to acting mindfully, rather than simply reacting instinctively. You're taking significant steps along the path of mindfulness. As Carla Naumberg states in her book, Parenting in the Present Moment: How to Stay Focused on What Really Matters: 'Mindful parenting isn't about what we do, it's about the awareness we bring to the choices we make.' Having done this once, you'll be able to do it again. Each time you do, you'll be teaching your brain to respond to tense situations with love and thoughtfulness.

Children and teens, with their undeveloped lateral prefrontal cortex, are even more under the sway of their emotions than adults. Teaching S.T.O.P to your children or your class is an invaluable way to help them deal with often overwhelming emotional cues. With smaller kids, Naumberg suggests a simplified version: Stop, Drop, Breathe. Play up the physical nature of it. Hold your hands up for 'Stop.' Throw yourself (safely) onto the floor for 'Drop.' And take deep, exaggerated breaths for 'Breathe', encouraging your kids to roll around with you. Don't underestimate the importance of fun in learning—or in mindfulness! Next time you discover your children having a yelling match in their bedroom or your students arguing, invite them to Stop, Drop, Breathe, before proceeding.

Guided Meditation Resources

Apps

Although constantly buzzing smartphones might seem like the antithesis of mindfulness, there are a number of guided meditation apps that are very useful. The following is a non-exclusive list of some that are out there.

Smiling Mind not only features programs designed specifically for children, but those programs are tailored for different developmental stages and the challenges that children face at different points of their school life. As a non-profit dedicated to improving the mental health and well-being of Australians through preemptive education and mindfulness practices, Smiling Mind not only has a wealth of research behind it but is being taught to a million school children across Australia. The free app has dozens of guided meditations suitable for ages seven through adult, and the blog shares the experiences of not only educators and advocates, but the students themselves. It is an amazing mindfulness resource for kids, teens, parents and teachers alike. Best of all, it is entirely free.

The UK developed app Buddhify lets you chose from a male or female voice and has a 'two-player' mode—perfect for getting your child involved. It has a few scenarios and can be used when out walking or at home.

32

Sleep Easily Meditation is, as its name suggests, focused on calming a busy mind for optimum sleep.

Simply Being Guided is another free meditation app aimed at beginners. It has a range of tips for novice meditators and allows you to customize your experience with different background noises.

Headspace is another app that always comes highly recommended. It was developed by a Buddhist monk, Andy Puddicombe. Andy's no-nonsense approach to meditation is occasionally lightened by humor, making headspace a hit with an audience that includes Emma Watson. The first sessions are free, and you can subscribe to unlock further meditations. Or you can simply go back and repeat the sessions as needed. Many find it useful without ever needing to unlock the paid content.

Other

We may be living in the electronic age, but don't overlook your local library as a resource for learning about mindfulness. You'll find books, audio-guides and possibly even video devoted to meditation techniques. If you can't find what you're looking for, ask your librarian about the possibility of borrowing from wider library systems.

Is there a yoga school in your neighborhood? Many yoga practitioners offer classes in meditation and may already be accustomed to teaching kids and teenagers. If you are able to find a teacher for your kids, ask if they'd mind you joining the session. You can observe how they teach to get an idea of how to go about helping your children at home. If there is no class for kids, ask about a private session for your family or if the practitioner would be interested in visiting your school (with the school's permission, of course!).

The internet is a wonderful resource. There are many guided meditation and mindful yoga videos freely available on Youtube. In fact, you may find the choice overwhelming! Get your kids involved to find a teacher that you will all enjoy.

Walking Meditation

Introduction to Walking Meditation

Walking meditation is exactly what it sounds like. You turn your attention inward, still focusing on your breath and body. The difference is that your body is in motion and your environment changing, bringing new challenges to your meditation practice.

There are multiple ways to practice walking meditation. Experiment until you find what works best for you and your child. If you need help getting started, Walking Meditations is an app that provides guided meditation to listen to as you walk.

Walking meditation is ideally combined in a quiet, calm environment—a quiet hiking track through glorious mountain scenery encourages mindfulness without us even making an effort, for example. But while we might be able to indulge in the occasional hike on a long weekend, our everyday reality may involve busy streets, uneven concrete paths, pedestrians and other hazards of city living. Don't let these put you off trying walking meditation. By bringing your awareness to your surroundings, you may discover the beauty you've overlooked in your own neighborhood.

You don't necessarily have to take your walking meditation outside. Buddhist monks practice meditation while pacing the length of temple rooms. You can do the same in your hall or the school gym. Walking indoors allows you to experiment with walking with shoes on or off. You don't necessarily need a big space either. You can walk in small or big circles—around your kitchen table, for example. Move furniture that might trip an unwary meditator out of the way and you're ready to begin.

Simple Walking Meditation (all ages, five to ten minutes)

Start by standing comfortably, with your arms by your side. Your back is straight and your shoulders are relaxed. Take a few moments to settle into your body. Pay careful attention to your feet. If doing this with younger children, ask them to imagine themselves as a tree or mountain, standing tall, but connected to the earth.

Focus on your breathing. If you like, you can close your eyes. You don't have to keep them closed for the full duration—and if you are walking outside, it might be a better idea to keep them open.

When you are ready, turn your focus to your feet. Let your mind gently explore the sensations in your toes and your ankles. Pay attention to where your foot meets the floor, and how the surface feels beneath your feet.

Shift all your weight onto one foot. Slowly raise the other, bending your knee. Adjusting your weight to stay balanced, move forward, placing your raised foot on the floor, and noting how the heel of the other foot raises. Shift your weight onto your forward foot, and repeat the process.

You're probably walking stiffly, like a robot! Relax, leaning into the familiarity of the motion of walking. Just like when you use breath as the basis of a meditation, your steps should be a focal point, not a distraction. If you or your child finds it difficult, try walking slowly, focusing on your breathing instead.

Continue to walk, back and forth or in circles, until you are ready to stop.

Walking Meditation Variations

On the go

You probably do plenty of walking in your everyday lives. The next time you're out and about with your child, take a few deep breaths and bring your awareness into your walk. Notice the sounds around you—passing cars, the murmur of conversation, the difference between your footsteps and that of your child. Look around as you walk. You may be surprised to notice what you see when you really pay attention. Afterward, compare notes with your child. What new thing did they notice? Did they experience any surprises on the walk?

You Always Take the Weather With You

Instead of complaining about the weather, experience it. Instead of delaying your walk because of the weather, pay attention to the sensations it produces. Feel the breeze running through your hair, the sun on your arms and legs, or the drizzle of the rain on your face. Dress appropriately, and open yourself to the different sensations each type of weather brings with it.

Breathing

This is good for younger children, or if you have trouble combining mindfulness and walking. Breathe in on one step, out on the other and repeat. In time, this will feel as natural as sitting meditation.

Athlete's foot, leg, arm and everything else

This practice is especially good for budding athletes, sports teams, or any situation where bodily performance is key. Begin the walking meditation as usual and once you're settled into your rhythm, perform a body scan (see Sitting Meditation: Simple Body Awareness Scan). Bring your attention to each part of your body, in turn, noticing how it moves, feels, and any tenseness, soreness or any other sensation. Continue bringing your attention to each part of your body in turn.

Professional athletes use this in training to hone their performance. Many marathon runners use this technique to stay focused while they run long distances. By paying attention to what your body is telling you rather than mindlessly repeating the same movement, you gain a greater awareness of your body and are able to fine-tune your movements, dealing with any problems as they arise rather than when they become too serious to ignore.

Object Meditation

Introduction to Object Meditation

You've already been introduced to object meditation. In sitting meditation, we start by focusing on the breath or body, in walking meditation with our feet. Object meditation brings what we already know to bear on an external object.

Choose your object. Preferably it is something small and ordinary, that you see and use every day without giving it a second thought. Good examples include a piece of food, such as a raisin, an apple, or a piece of chocolate, a leaf or a flower, or even a coin.

Settle yourself comfortably in a sitting position with your object beside you. When you're ready, close your eyes. Take three deep breaths, deeper than you normally would. When you've done this, count ten regular breaths.

Open your eyes. Take the object of your meditation in your hand. Notice its weight and how it feels in your hand. Roll it around in your hands. Pay attention to its texture. Is it smooth, rough? Are there any imperfections in its surface? Does it feel cold or has it taken on your body heat?

Now, hold the object up to your eyes and examine it closely. Note the color and if it changes. Look at the object from different angles. Try and see it as if you're seeing it for the first time.

Hold the object to your ear. Does it have a sound? Try shaking it or tapping it with your finger.

Hold the object to your nose. What is its smell? Notice where in the nose you feel the smell. Is it earthy? Sweet? Does it remind you of anything?

If the object is edible, now is the moment to taste it. Put it in your mouth or take a bite. Notice how it feels in your mouth before you start to chew. As you chew, pay attention to how your teeth work and the taste. Where on your tongue do you taste it most? When you swallow, notice the taste left in your mouth.

When you're ready, finish the meditation by closing your eyes and taking three deep breaths. Hold the object in your mind. Remember any insights you gained about it and thank the object for teaching you.

Writing Meditation

Introduction to Writing Meditation

As with sitting and walking meditation, there are as many ways to practice mindful writing as there are types of children. There is no one size fits all.

When we use breathing to anchor our meditation practice, we're drawing on something we've been doing since the very moment our lives began. We've been walking for longer than we can remember. The fact that both of these things are so deeply ingrained that we no longer notice we're doing them unless prompted makes them a good basis for meditation.

Writing is learned later in life and never becomes fully automatic. We still have to think about what we want to say before we can form words on the page. For this reason, writing meditations work differently to sitting or walking meditation, being more of a reflective tool rather than a true meditation technique—with two notable exceptions.

Copying Meditation

Shakyo is the Japanese term for the practice of copying out Buddhist sutras. I first encountered this when visiting Kokudera temple in Kyoto with my sister. Admission to the temple included attending a service with the monks, followed by sitting at a low desk, tracing kanji figures with a brush. We were there to see the temple's famous moss garden, not study Buddhism. I could read a few of the Kanji and knew what order to write the strokes in. It was my sister's first time to visit Japan, and the symbols had even less meaning for her. Yet, we both found that we felt a sense of peace from applying ourselves to tracing the sutras. This writing meditation is good for kids with a tendency towards learning by doing or in situations where a walking meditation is impossible.

Instead of hunting down Buddhist sutras, I suggest helping your child decide on a motto or an inspiring phrase, and making that the object of their meditation (I like 'Imagination is more important than knowledge. Knowledge is limited. Imagination encircles the world'— Albert Einstein). Devote five to ten minutes to writing out that phrase. As you do, focus on it the same way you focus on your breathing or your movements when walking. Notice the smell of the paper, the sound of your pen. Encourage your child to bring a sense of wonder to the exercise—if it feels like a chore or a punishment, move on to a different form of meditation.

Drawing Meditation

One important aspect of mindfulness is seeing a familiar object in a new way. In her ground-breaking book, Drawing on the Right Side of the Brain, Betty Edwards came up with an exercise to help artists break out of preconceived ideas and see what was before their eyes— triggering the 'flow' state that many creatives (artists, writers, performers) aspire to. This flow state is the end goal of meditation. While Betty Edwards may not know it, but I believe she is teaching mindfulness through the following drawing exercise.

Take a familiar picture—something with clearly defined lines is best. Rather than a photo, choose a black and white sketch or a print. Turn it upside down. Taking a fresh piece of paper, copy the upside down picture exactly as you see it. Resist the urge to turn it right way up, or to turn your paper around. Just keep drawing, using the distance and angle between lines guide your drawing. Only compare the pictures when your drawing meditation practice is complete.

Use this meditation with kids who are still learning or who struggle to write, or have a strong interest in art, or in using their hands.

Writing Meditation

This exercise is the most commonly accepted form of writing meditation. Simply sit down with a pen, a blank piece of paper and a timer and see what happens. Don't self-edit or think about what you're writing. Simply let the words flow. The idea is to write so quickly that your brain doesn't have time to censor itself. The results may surprise you.

If you find that following a formal structure helps you and/or your child, then you might find this guideline for writing meditation developed by Jane Brunette, writing and meditation teacher.

Start your meditation practice by sitting at your desk. Take a moment to settle into your posture. Check that you have pen, paper and a timer, and that your chair supports you. When you're ready, focus on your breathing. Spend at least five minutes on a simple breathing meditation, or count twenty-one breaths. Now you're ready to begin.

Set your timer for ten minutes (adjust depending on the attention span of your child). Start with the words 'Right now' and follow with whatever comes into your mind. Don't edit, try to lead the sentence towards a conclusion, or stop to make corrections. Just write. When you finish what you're saying, start again with another 'right now.' Don't give yourself time to think. Write. Don't censor the words as they come out. It's okay to be surprised.

When the timer goes off, take a few deep breaths. Put the pen down and pick up your paper. Look at what you've written. Read it out loud if you're alone. If doing this with a child, read silently, and don't read your child's writing. Privacy is crucial to this exercise—if your child is worried about what you'll think of their writing, they won't be free to express their subconscious minds.

Pick up your pen again. Read through your writing, underlining any words that stand out. Maybe they are unexpected, maybe they resonate, maybe they're repeated throughout your writing. Or maybe it simply intrigues you (if this is the case, consider saving it for another writing session).

Reflect on what discoveries you've made through your writing practice. Resolve to act on them, or make the wish that whatever insight you've gained will have a positive impact on your life and that of those around you.

Mindful Journalling

Using a journal can help you improve your mindfulness practice. There are two main ways to use your mindfulness journal. You can make it part of your practice, by writing in your journal after your daily meditation practice or as part of your preparing for bed routine, or you can use it to record your progress on your journey towards mindfulness.

Reflective Journalling

The very act of keeping a journal encourages mindfulness. By recording their daily events, your child becomes naturally aware that there are good days and bad, and that emotions come and go. However, by making it a habit to write in a journal after meditation, you cement the insights gained through your meditation into your consciousness. If your child prefers to meditate on their own, their journal (should they allow you to read it), provides you with a record of their progress, and an insight into what struggles they're having with meditation and may help you offer guidance. If you're a teacher with a class of mindful students, these journals will be invaluable to assess the needs of your class and help you provide the most effective guidance.

Mindfulness Tracking

Keeping a record of your progress can be incredibly motivating. This doesn't have to be very involved. The date, time spend in mindful practice, what insight you gained, your feeling of well-being before and after are all you need. Many meditation apps, Smiling Mind, for example, allow you to assess your happiness, contentedness, and calm before and after each exercise, logging results so that you can view the effect of meditation on your mood over time. For younger children, encourage them to draw a simple picture representing their mood before and after each day's meditation.

Mindfulness at School

In exploring meditation, we've already touched on ways mindfulness can be incorporated into a child's life at home or at school. To prevent repetition, rather than focusing on how to use meditation at home or in the classroom, we're going to explore other ways that a mindful awareness will benefit kids and teens.

Whether you're a parent, teacher, youth leader or coach, I recommend reading both the at school and at home sections. With a little imagination, I'm sure you'll see how the underlying ideas in each section can be adapted to your situation in order to teach mindfulness to the kids and teens in your life.

Mindfulness at School

The benefits of starting both the school day and each class with a short meditation to focus students' attention have already been discussed in this book. The benefits of incorporating mindful precepts into education don't stop there. Taking a mindful perspective into learning can greatly broaden students' understanding of themselves, the subject and their worldview. These bold claims are backed up by extensive research done by Ellen J. Langer, during the course of her forty-year career in psychology. Langer writes about the benefits of a mindful perspective at length in her seminal book Mindfulness, and the following is a brief summary of the ideas most useful to teachers, or home-schooling parents.

Traditional Education: Can I do it?

Traditional education focuses more on goals than on processes. Although there are exceptions to this rule, for the most part, children are presented with questions for which there is a right and wrong answer. Tests are passed or failed. The effect of this binary divisions is that children grow up assuming that for every decision they make there is a right answer and a wrong answer. Have you been faced with an innocuous decision like where to go for dinner with a friend, and throughout the dinner, found yourself evaluating your choice of restaurant with either congratulation or regret? This is a symptom of thinking in dualities, and it permeates much of how we interact with the world. If we are 'right,' other people's opinions must be 'wrong.' Although this may seem an oversimplification, consider how much of the political rhetoric of today builds of the divide between opposing schools of thought rather than seeking common ground.

This duality also has a harmful effect on students self-image. It encourages students to constantly evaluate themselves and their peers. Students place themselves in categories such as 'smart' 'funny' or 'sporty'—or more harmful categories such as 'loser.' Once having placed themselves, students cling to assumptions rather than questioning them. They may make little effort to explore talents that lie outside of their category, instead focusing on what lies within their self-defined limits. Their behavior becomes automatic, reflexive rather than reflective. When they make decisions, they do so from a single perspective and are more likely to see differences of opinion, behavior, appearance or culture as a threat to personal attack.

A Mindful Perspective: How do I do it?

A mindful perspective shifts the focus from the goals to the process. Instead of 'can I do it?' a mindful approach to learning encourages students to think 'how do I do it?' When looking at the lives of athletes, scientists, activists and other individuals in the classroom, look at the exact steps that person took to get where they are today or to achieve what they did. Demystifying success and breaking it down into building blocks helps students see that success is a replicable process. Encourage students to look closely at the lives of their heroes and help them research people working in fields they're interested in. Shifting from a 'can I' to a 'how do I' mindset could be the single most important change in a student's life.

Mindfulness, with its focus on bringing awareness and attention to objects and thoughts that are usually accepted without question naturally fosters a more tolerant approach to difference. You can build on this in the classroom. Successive studies that Langer and her students undertook in schools discovered that students who participated in exercises where they were encouraged to come up with multiple labels or explanations for a picture or a scenario behaved with more tolerance and understanding than students who were asked to come up with one 'right answer.' By encouraging students to think beyond their first assumptions, teachers can lay the foundations for greater understanding throughout the student's life.

The benefits of this mindful perspective are many. Instead of categorizing themselves and the people they encounter into a few narrowly defined categories, mindful thinkers constantly create new, specific categories, adapting to context rather than rigidly clinging to preconceived ideas. Mindful thinkers welcome new information and are able to take other's perspectives into account when making decisions. They're not hampered by the belief that there is one right answer or by a need to 'win.' They feel empowered, knowing that facts are dependent on context and that they are not bound by preconceptions of who they are. Most importantly of all, they value the process rather than the outcome, understanding that success in their chosen field is within their grasp.

Teaching mindful thinking doesn't mean throwing the old curriculum out. Mindful teachers focus on the process of passing tests rather than the outcome to motivate students, while mindful parents can show their children that they are more than the sum of their academic achievements. As Naumburg states in Parenting in the Present Moment: How to Stay Focused on What Really Matters, it is important to praise effort rather than outcome. Instead of saying 'that's a good picture,' say 'I can see that you worked really hard on this picture.' In this way, children learn to value hard work and determination, and avoid type-casting themselves as good or bad at certain activities.

The value of Mindful Thinking Beyond the Classroom.

Not convinced that mindful thinking is a skill that will benefit young children? Perhaps the interest in bringing mindfulness into the workplace will convince you. Many major corporations have seen the benefits that employees who are less stressed, more productive, and able to think outside of the box bring to the workplace and are actively incorporating mindfulness into their business culture. For example, ever since 2007, Google has been running mindfulness courses taken by thousands of employees every year. The most popular, the 'Search Inside Yourself' course, has a waiting list of six months. Employees describe it as 'life-changing,' but Google's motives are not altruistic. As Chade Meng-Tan, who developed Google's mindfulness programs told WIRED, "every company knows that if their people have [Emotional Intelligence], they're going to make a shitload of money."

Bringing imagination and compassion to business decisions is a skill that is increasingly in demand, no matter what field your child or students want to work in. Mindfulness and mindful thinking, in particular, will not only help students achieve better results academically, but it will make them more motivated, more passionate, more creative, and more well-rounded people.

Mindfulness at Home

Just as an infant's interactions with their parents influences their brain development, home-life has a lifelong influence on many aspects of our children's lives. Since we see our children at home every day and interactions become routine, it is easy to forget how important and meaningful these moments with our children are. Spend a moment reflecting on moments from your childhood that have stayed with you for good or for bad, and you will be surprised at home many of them are small, everyday occurrences.

Carla Naumburg's Parenting in the Present Moment is a fantastic resource for mindful parenting, and I highly recommend reading for the insight, compassion, and humor she brings to the subject. Here are just a few ways of bringing mindfulness into your home life.

Mindful Eating

Sitting down to share a meal together as a family is one of the most important things you can do for your children. This time spent doesn't only foster relationships and keep you up to date with the important events of your child's life, but it informs their relationship to food throughout their life. As Naumburg states: 'Research has found a range of benefits to sharing meals together, such as lower rates of drug use and behavioral problems, better grades, and higher self-esteem, benefits you might expect from children who regularly connect with their families in meaningful ways.' The key is making mealtime meaningful. Dinner works best for most families, but if breakfast is the only time that your family is reliably together, get up earlier to make breakfast less rushed.

Your family may already have a habit of saying 'grace' before the meal. If so, build on this to include thanks for the good things that have happened throughout the day. Or you might prefer to start the meal with a few moments spent in mindful eating (see object meditation). However, while mindful eating uses the act of eating to focus awareness on the sensations of eating, you don't want to miss out on the chance to connect with your child. Make the focus of the meal on connecting with your family. Make it a family rule not to bring electronics into the dining room, and adhere to it yourself. If your mind wanders while your children or your spouse talks about their day, bring your attention firmly back to the moment at hand, just as you would in meditation practice. This brings us to mindful listening.

Mindful Listening

Too often our attention wanders while we're in conversation with someone. We fall into autopilot mode, making the appropriate responses while our minds wander. How often have you found that you've zoned out while a friend talks, only to be jerked back to the conversation with the realization that they're waiting for a response that you've got no idea how to make? Or do you listen to the conversation, while evaluating what has been said, mentally rehearsing your reply, or wondering what an appropriate response to make is? In either situation, we're doing ourselves and our conversational partner a disservice by not investing our full awareness into listening.

Listening mindfully is simply listening. When thoughts or feelings spring into our minds, we notice them and let them go, applying our attention to our child's words. Instead of hearing what we think they're saying, we open ourselves to hearing what they're really saying. Instead of framing a suitable response, or worrying whether or not our face is showing the 'right' emotion (see how insidious that duality of thinking is?), we accept what we hear without judgment. In doing so, we give the person speaking permission to be themselves and express themselves fully.

Mindful listening does not mean accepting whatever you hear without question. As you turn your full awareness to your conversational partner, you'll notice clues to their mood and state of mind in their facial expression and their movements. You may feel an emotional response—perhaps even anger—to what the speaker says, but you'll recognize your response, and will be less likely to react emotionally. Being attentive and truly present in a conversation will greatly enrich

Even when we disagree, mindfully listening to someone is one of the greatest gifts you can give someone. Try it out with your child or spouse. Explain what listening mindfully entails, and when you're ready, sit down comfortably somewhere you can see each other clearly. Decide who will speak first and set a timer for two or three minutes. The listener asks 'what makes you happy?' As the speaker talks, the listener resists the urge to react with questions, facial expressions, and simply applies their attention to the speaker's words. Like in meditation practice, they notice how their attention wanders. They observe their thoughts and emotions, and let go of them, bring their attention back to the moment. When the timer goes or the speaker is finished, swap roles. When you've both spoken, you can share your experiences.

Mindful chores

It can be a struggle to find time for mindfulness among the busy schedule of school, sports activities, homework and social arrangements of your child. If your child has chores they do as a matter of routine, whether on a daily or weekly basis, encourage them to turn the chore into a mindful meditation. This has the benefit of associating mindfulness with some part of the child's routine, making mindfulness a regular part of their life. This works best with repetitive tasks that are easy to do on autopilot. Washing dishes, folding clothes, putting up laundry, raking the leaves, washing the car or walking the dog are all possibilities. If you're a teacher looking for mindful tasks for your students, consider making tidying up the classroom at the end of the day a part of your routine, or applying this to another monotonous physical activity, such as going for a walk as a class.

The goal is to bring mindfulness back to a task that is so routine that the child does not need their full attention to do it. Usually, their mind drifts and while performing the task, will be mentally occupied with plans for the weekend, worrying about what a friend thinks of them or other preoccupations. To help them do the task mindfully, join them in it. Start with a few deep breaths as in formal meditation practice, and then begin the activity. For younger children, direct their attention to the various stages of the activity. For older children, challenge them to notice something new about the experience. Just like in meditation, apply yourself to the task, pulling your mind back to what you're doing every time it wanders. You'll finish the chore with a sense of wellbeing and relaxation that you'll carry into the rest of your day.

Mindfulness Habit

Like any skill or muscle, the more you exercise mindfulness, the easier and more natural it becomes. In the meditation section, I talked about the impact even a short daily meditation makes, while in the Mindfulness at School and Mindfulness at Home sections, we touched on ways to bring mindfulness into everyday classroom and home situations. You've probably already got ideas on how to bring mindfulness into your child's life or into your classroom. Here we look at strategies for making sure that your good intentions become a daily habit.

The easiest way to develop a new habit is to incorporate it into something you already do. For example, if you want to use mindfulness to help you sleep better, look for ways to incorporate mindfulness into your pre-bedtime routine by looking at your existing routine. If brushing your teeth is the last thing you do before bed, then apply your attention to mindfully brushing your teeth.

Once your new habit has become part of your routine (about three weeks), extend it. Perhaps after brushing your teeth mindfully, you add a five-minute meditation. Over time, you can gradually extend the time you spend on your pre-bed meditation.

Schedule time for mindfulness the same way that you set aside time for meetings, extra-curricular activities, and social events. Put them in your diary, set alerts on your phone and protect your time. If you are meditating for longer, you may need to bring your bedtime forward, for example.

Reward perseverance. Place a sticker on a calendar or check off a box to show that you've met your goal. Children enjoy seeing checkmarks or stickers accumulate, and you may be surprised at how satisfying it feels to mark off another box. If you miss a day, instead of berating yourself, focus on the next day. Watch your inner dialogue. Instead of reacting with 'I failed,' tell yourself 'it's not like me to forget to meditate. I will be sure not to let it happen again tomorrow, and will set a phone alarm to remind me.' If you'd prefer not to offer a material reward for perseverance, focus instead on the benefits your daily mindfulness practice will bring you.

Tracking your progress isn't just satisfying. It helps you to understand your habits better. You'll be more aware of your strengths and your weaknesses. You will spot patterns and learn what situations are likely to disrupt your new mindfulness practice and come up with solutions to counter them. If Thursday is always really busy because of school activities and you get home exhausted, then perhaps settle for simply mindfully brushing your teeth on Thursdays, and adding an extra five minutes of meditation to Wednesday or Friday's routine, or perhaps finding another time on Thursday to practice mindfulness.

The most important thing in practicing mindfulness is to be flexible. Mindfulness should never be demanding or prescriptive. Just as you, your children, and your classes are all unique and have different needs, hopes and aspirations, your mindfulness practice will be different—and will change over time as you and your children grow. The good news is that by practicing mindfulness, you will be practicing your self-awareness and constantly attuning yourself to your mental state, so you'll be equipped to figure out what you need when you need it.

Made in the USA
Lexington, KY
30 November 2017